Poetry in (e)motion:
the illustrated words of Scroobius Pip

Titan Books

poetry in (e)motion

The illustrated words of Scroobius Pip

ISBN: 9781848566170

Published by Titan Books, a division of Titan Publishing Group Ltd. 144 Southwark St, London, SE1 0UP

Strip credits: Anthony Gregori – 1000 Words; Joe Cunningham (pigflaps) – When I Grow Up; Damian
Claughton – Reading My Dreams; Inna Aizenshtein – Magician's Assistant; Colin McCracken – Ode to a B-
Boy; Matthew Frodsham – Waiting for the Beat To Kick In; Ben Williams – Thou Shalt Always Kill; Scott
Paterson – Shamed; Suzanne Williams (cowfree) – Rat Race.

A CIP catalogue record for this title is available from the British Library.

This edition first published: March 2010

10 9 8 7 6 5 4

Printed in China

What did you think of this book? We'd love to hear from our readers.
Please email us at readerfeedback@titanemail.com, or write to us at the above address.

I would like to thank my mum, dad, brother and girlfriend for all their support, dan le sac for continuing to push and motivate me, Nick Frost for his
rhyme skills, Katy Wild, David Leach, Martin Stiff, Ricky Claydon and everyone at Titan and Sunday Best for helping me get this book made, Jaimie
Knott for inspiring me long, long ago and, most importantly of all, every single artist that submitted work and turned a load of ramblings on my hard
drive into my first ever publication. Pip

Contents:

and thats your lot!

SCROOB

P.I.P

- i can't draw hats...

Paul McDonald, Oddsock Illustration. www.oddsockillustration.com

foreword by
Nick Frost

When Pip asked me to write the foreword to his excellent book
I said sure, I'll take a look.
I's always been a fan
and this was a real honour for a 38 year old man.
I asked if he wanted me to do it as a rhyme,
he said, 'No.' Just a few words describing the book would be fine.
So here's mine.
I did it as a rhyme, I hope you don't mind?
It's like *Avatar* for the HipHop generation,
It's a 3rd gen Playstation.
It's Bacardi and Coke,
It's a long, deep toke.
It's *Where Eagles Dare*.
It's the soft, quick feet of Fred Astaire.
It's bacon and eggs,
It's long brown legs.
It's slow cooked stew,
It's me and it's you.
It's sunrise and star shine,
Drawings and def rhyme.
It's a fabulous book
and I implore you, take a look.
And soon you will see
that Scroobius Pip is the one for me.
(I mean lyrically.)

So to recap... ENJOY!!!

Cheers all.

NICK FROST

Introduction

I NEVER really read much poetry when I was a kid. In school it seemed too hard to get your head round and I think the mistake that schools make is to immediately focus on "the classics". A lot of the language used, whilst beautiful, is very different from the modern dialect and I think it would make more sense to ease children in and let them enjoy walking around the language first before trying to march them over tougher terrain.

My introduction to poetry and spoken word came through necessity as much as anything else. As a teen I had always been passionate about music. Punk ignited my passion, then Hip Hop and Jazz and after that, pretty much any other genre I could get my ears round just kept the fire burning. As my interest grew the only logical progression was to buy a guitar. Straight away I was forming little punk bands that never really wrote much or played many gigs or had much skill but despite that, they were DEFINITELY bands. I learnt pretty quickly that the worst thing about bands was trying to organise everyone! Drummers can never get their drum kits to practice rooms or gigs. Bassists always have to be home in time for dinner or their mothers get furious. And guitarists just drink too much or do too many drugs to really have any specific, consistent traits. This realisation came at a time when I was listening to more and more spoken word artists like Gil Scott Heron, Sage Francis and Saul Williams. It was through their own mixing of genres and styles that it occurred to me that if I took up the spoken word as my medium, I wouldn't have to rely on band mates! I liked the thought of having no one else to blame but yourself and the idea that it was all up to me was both appealing and daunting. If I took up spoken word and failed miserably, it would be my fault alone.

i never really read much poetry when i was a kid

I was working in a record shop at the time (2002ish) and I decided to start saving my money and writing. By the time I had written enough to have a decent spoken word set I had saved enough money to live/exist for a year without an income. I promptly quit my job and toured around the country living in a 1987 Toyota Space Cruiser. The plan was to go out on the streets with a mic, a speaker and my words, but I rapidly learned that town centres weren't necessarily filled with what I would call my target audience. Luckily I'm not one to give in quickly and I decided that the first thing I needed to do, when arriving in a new town, was to look up the gig listings for that night. Over the weeks, acts like Buck 65, Atmosphere, DJ Shadow and many more, literally lined my potential audiences up against walls to listen to me while they queued. All I had to do was turn up and try to win them over.

I received mixed reactions.

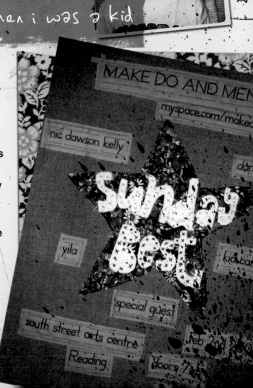

MAKE DO AND MEN

myspace.com/maked

nic dawson kelly

dan

sunday best

yila

kidxca

special guest

south street arts centre
Reading.

After a month or two of crossing the country I returned home and decided to focus exclusively on London and Essex. I would attend, on average, four or five spoken word shows a week. Open mic nights, slams and anywhere where I thought there was a chance I would be able to get on stage and perform.

Within a few months I was starting to get fairly regular gigs. It certainly didn't hurt that I had a massive beard, some second-hand suits and a trucker cap (all of which help you stand out at spoken word shows).

One of the bonuses of a growing profile was I suddenly had producers willing to work with me. I talked to several of them who all seemed really talented but the one that really stood out for me just happened to be an old workmate from my record shop days: dan le sac [sic]. From the first time I listened to his work, it was clear he had a style all of his own and after doing a couple of gigs and remixes together, we decided to have a go at writing some new tracks and about a month after that we were getting played on national radio and touring the country!

The combination of dan's musical style and my spoken word delivery just seemed to gel and together we made a kind of hip hop (if it is even that) that seemed to stand out and sound different from almost everything else being recorded.

The next year or two was a whirlwind. I got to perform my work on national radio stations, in London clubs at 3am, halfway up a Japanese mountain, to crowds of thousands at festivals all over the UK and Europe, to a crowd of around 200 people at my local library and in countless other unimaginable situations.

My introduction to poetry and spoken word came through necessity as much as anything else

From quite early on in this little adventure I had people asking me if I would ever release a book of poetry. The problem I had with that idea was… well, was what I said in my opening line of this foreword!

I never really read much poetry as a kid. And, to be honest, I still don't read that much now. I prefer to watch or hear it performed live by the poets themselves.

It just seemed arrogant to me to put out a book of your own poetry. It felt like I would be saying, "There's no poetry out there worth ME reading but YOU should definitely read MY poetry!" It just didn't sit well with me. So if I was to release a book of my poetry I wanted to do so in a way that would maybe make it more appealing to people, like myself, people who hadn't read much of it when they were children.

At a gig, quite early on, someone gave me a philosophy essay to read that had been written and drawn like a short comic book. I thought it was great how well it got all the points across yet didn't seem like a chore to read. Now, obviously, I am prepared for any "dumbing" down arguments to come up at this point! But I truly believe that any medium that can ignite an interest in something, for someone who might otherwise have been out of reach is perfectly valid.

And so it was here that I came up with the concept for this collection.

In 2007 I put out a message on MySpace asking for artists and illustrators who might be interested in working on a little project with me. I had put together a shortlist of poems and the idea was to get different artists from all over the world to submit works that were interpretations of those pieces. The only rule was that the poem had to be included within the artwork, in full and unabridged. Other than that it was the proverbial empty canvas!

Now, the problem with social networking sites is, you can have 1000s of "friends" but you never really know if any one of them is actually paying attention and I really didn't know what kind of reaction, if any, I would get. I shouldn't have worried, within the first few days I had thirty to forty people contacting me asking to take part and this number just grew and grew over the next year or two until I had hundreds of submissions from all over the world. I had made it clear to everyone who contacted me that they might not make it into the final book but that I was grateful to all of them regardless. And I truly was! To see this reaction to a load of poems I had written in my little town of Stanford le Hope in Essex was frankly amazing and I took great pride and pleasure in looking through every single entry. Some entries came from people that, from our email exchanges, clearly didn't speak much English and yet were willing to take on this task and some came from people who just submitted any old paintings or picture they'd had lying around that they claimed were interpretations of one of my poems… cheeky.

with in the first few days I had 30-40 people contacting me asking to take part.

It's only when I started to prepare samples to show to publishers that I quite realised what a great collection I had amassed. Somehow the variation of all the different approaches just seemed to work so well and I was pleased to see that a weird little idea I'd had several years before now suddenly felt complete.

I want to take this opportunity to thank every single person that submitted a piece whether we used it or not. If we could have included all the entries then we would have (although you probably wouldn't enjoy going through them in quite the same way as I did).

To finally get to release this book at the end of such an epic journey feels fantastic! And I hope you enjoy reading it as much as I enjoyed compiling it (and as much as I hope each amazing artist enjoyed illustrating it).

Scroobius Pip

Stanford le Hope 2009

Scroobius Pip, Angles 2009 by Leigh Glover, Oil on canvas, 145 x 110cm. www.leighglover.com

1000 words

THIS really seemed like the only logical place to start this little collection. *1000 Words* was the first piece I wrote that made me think that perhaps this writing lark might be something more than just a hobby. It was also one of the first recordings I put up online and to me it was clearly the stand-out track on my debut solo album *No Commercial Breaks*.

I had come up with the idea of writing a poem that was EXACTLY 1000 words in length and this seemed like a good story to tell. As with most stories, it's part autobiographical and part abstract fiction. It's about an incident that happened to me when I was a child that was responsible for me developing a stutter.

Not having the ability to say certain words with ease kind of forces you to find replacements thus ironically broadening your vocabulary through necessity rather than any artistic choice. In a very real way you actually lose, or at least have restrictions placed upon, your freedom of speech. A right that we are lucky enough to take for granted.

As with most stories, it's part autobiographical part abstract fiction.

For some reason it just never felt like a "live" piece and I never felt comfortable performing it live. The length and pace of it felt that it should be enjoyed by the listener in their own time rather than thrust upon them on a night out!

The first time I tried it out live was at a small poetry night in a London bar and whilst people seemed to be enjoying it, about halfway through I knew it wasn't going to have a regular slot in my live sets. It's strange how that can happen.

This was the first submission I got after I put my request for artists on MySpace and it made me realise the potential of the collection. The art details were amazing and it took a friend of mine to point out that the monument and street scene on the first page were taken from my hometown of Stanford le Hope, Essex!

With this being an American submission that kind of dedication and attention to detail blew me away. The fact that someone from so far away had researched details in such a way truly humbled me.

Over the next few months I received small segments a piece at a time. At one point I was tempted to just say "Send me the final piece when it's all done!" Not out of anger or frustration but simply because the anticipation built by each trickling incarnation was almost too much to handle!

When it all finally came through and I got to see it as one complete submission, I knew I had my starting point.

Anthony Gregori
PENCILLER

ANTHONY GREGORI was born and raised in South Florida and studied Illustration at the Art Institute of Ft Lauderdale. He relocated to San Diego CA for a spell, only to return to the humidity and rain of Florida. He currently has several comic projects in development with reputable writers and creators. He would like it to be known that he is basically a lucky guy who loves what he does! ang76.daportfolio.com

Michael Spicer
COLOURIST

MICHAEL SPICER fell into colouring a couple of years ago. He is a self-taught artist who has been drawing since he was a kid. After years of trying a lot of other creative outlets/media and a several year hiatus from art altogether, Michael found himself creating again in a niche that he really enjoys! mspicer76.daportfolio.com

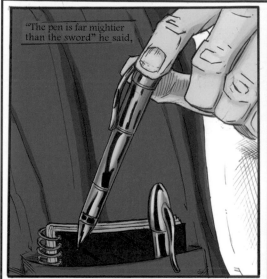

"The pen is far mightier than the sword" he said,

As he stabbed his pen in my leg and the ink mixed with the RED.

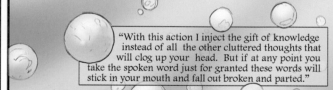

"With this action I inject the gift of knowledge instead of all the other cluttered thoughts that will clog up your head. But if at any point you take the spoken word just for granted these words will stick in your mouth and fall out broken and parted."

It didn't hurt for some reason but I could feel a change inside. But I hadn't really understood what his words had implied I thought I'd wait for his next words with my mind open wide and with the guidelines that he gave me I would try to abide.

Again much time passed with silence being the topic. But serenity was such bliss I had no words that could stop it.

And so I went on with my life

these things locked up in my brain

grew up no different from the rest, everything just stayed the same.

Until one day I realised sometimes my own speech was erratic.

Like the needle on my record would get all caught up and static. And at school, this affliction didn't make things too easy.

An easy target so the kids would sometimes laugh at and tease me.

I guess there's no denying this made me stand out from the rest. But that kind of thing has never fazed me. I just took it in jest. Sure the broken stammers of a youth can kind of bring some attention

But the sympathy of a teacher can get you out of detention

And this continued until I reached a certain age. Until I started to thrive for knowledge from every word and every page. All of a sudden, the words would just flow off of my tongue. When I got bored of how one sounded I'd just learn a new one.

I started listening to all the people who showed great use of each word. Feeling the buzz with every single line from Gil that I heard.

The way he manipulated the language and really made it develop, As he told another story from 125th Street and Lenox

And Mr. Mojo rising the American poet

had enraptured my mind with words and would never know it. I would sit in my room for hours just listening out for every underlying meaning in the words he would shout.

Then Id put on
The Specials

to hear of
their
social commentary,

You couldn't help but get drawn in
sometimes even involuntary

And the way that Rakim
would take

my mind
on a
journey

To a kind of life style and scene
that never use to concern me

A completely different world
to the one that I lived in.

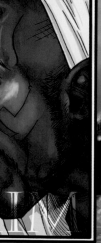

RAKIM

But I
could
connect
to the
language
and the
passion
within him

So I started to write, inspired by those here before me.

Id found an outlet for thoughts a way of telling a story

So I wrote

and I wrote

until I felt it was time to put some of this stuff on tape and then

I started to rhyme

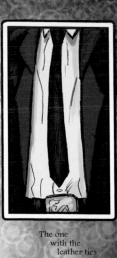

Once I started climbing I knew there was no way I could slip, And that was the one true birth of this here Scroobius Pip

The one with the leather ties

and weathered eyes

Who's
37 clever lines
left 37
severed minds
The one that speaks
but never lies.

And sometimes fails
but always tries.

And the more
he writes
the more he finds,
It pays to bleed
between the lines.

They say a picture's worth
a thousand words
so with these thousand words.

I'll paint a picture in your mind that breaks the rule of thirds.

They say a picture's worth
a thousand words
so with these thousand words.

I'll paint you one big picture
in your mind
that breaks the rule of thirds.

scroobius pip

the "relying on the kindness of strangers" tour 2006

no commercial breaks
released 25th april 2006

"finally a uk act in the vain of sage francis, saul williams and atmosphere" djbonrhyme

"eclectically covers hip-hop, jazz, punk and poetry...and thats just the parts that can be catagorized!" tzue

"is this serious?...i feel sorry for this artist. doesnt appeal to me in the slightest. crap." westwood

"great debut...big things ahead for this kid" www.bigappleflow.com

in may 2006 i am going to get in a van and start driving round the country. the rest is up to you. organizing an event? scroobius pip will perform. got a band? i'll do a track with you at your next gig. work in a book/coffee shop? i'll come and do an accapella set. got a radio show? i'll appear on it. i am open to suggestions! at worst i will tour the country and just perform on the streets, at best small children could learn to love again. the concept album is dead, long live the concept tour!

the "relying on the kindness of strangers" tour 2006

in may 2006 i am going to get in a van and start driving round the country. the rest is up to you. organizing an event? scroobius pip will perform. got a band? i'll do a track with you at your next gig. work in a book/coffee shop? i'll come and do an accapella set. got a radio show? i'll appear on it. i am open to suggestions! at worst i will tour the country and just perform on the streets, at best small children could learn to love again. the concept album is dead, long live the concept tour!

scroobius pip

no commercial breaks
released 25th april 2006

"finally a uk act in the vain of sage francis, saul williams and atmosphere" djbonrhyme

"eclectically covers hip-hop, jazz, punk and poetry...and thats just the parts that can be catagorized!" tzue

"is this serious?...i feel sorry for this artist. doesnt appeal to me in the slightest. crap." westwood

"great debut...big things ahead for this kid" www.bigappleflow.com

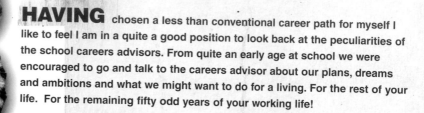

when i grow up

HAVING chosen a less than conventional career path for myself I like to feel I am in a quite a good position to look back at the peculiarities of the school careers advisors. From quite an early age at school we were encouraged to go and talk to the careers advisor about our plans, dreams and ambitions and what we might want to do for a living. For the rest of your life. For the remaining fifty odd years of your working life!

Now, I don't know about you, but when I was at school, I wasn't normally sure what I wanted to do the following weekend, let alone for the rest of my life!

There is, of course, nothing wrong with planning things out and building towards your personal goals and targets but I just feel that a lot of the time in education there is too much of an "achieve this or you have failed" attitude.

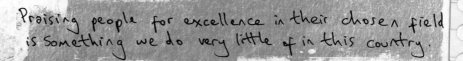

Praising people for excellence in their chosen field is something we do very little of in this country.

Joe Cunningham

PIGFLAPS is the alter ego of Joe Cunningham. Primarily using this secret identity to fight crime under the shroud of darkness, he also kills time scrawling puerile doodles on the back of cereal boxes for his own self-published comic and sporadic freelance illustration, lying gigantically to children and often doing himself a mischief, heroically attempting to consume his own body weight in Kit-Kat Chunkys. Pigflaps comics, etchings and other childish swearing can be found at pigflaps.wordpress.com and he can be contacted on pigflaps@gmail.com. Pigflaps does also not enjoy talking in the third person.

As a stuttering teen at school the idea that I would have CHOSEN to stand up in front of people and talk for a living would have seemed ridiculous, both to me and to my careers advisor and yet that's the path I chose for myself! Careers advice at a young age can also tend to turn it into a bit of a status competition. Very few kids at my school ever came out of the careers meeting proudly stating they were going to be a butcher or a baker and yet there are many valid and perfectly good jobs that aren't really shown as a good "target" to aim for. Rewarding and praising people for excellence in their chosen field is something we do very little of in this country, but manage to warble your way through some songs on a TV show and you will be applauded and called a star. Survive a reality show with only one or two disgracefully racist moments and you will be praised as a hero. Work hard six days a week, as a mechanic or milkman, and you rarely get a mention.

Before receiving this artwork the artist sent a copy of the fanzine he makes and distributes around Brighton. Having grown up loving punk and the DIY nature of its roots I really enjoyed his approach to getting his artwork out there.

When the submission came through it lived up to everything I had hoped for. Every frame seemed so busy but always necessarily so.

WHEN I GROW UP

SEE THE FRIENDS I MADE AND I WERE DIFFERENT FROM THE GET GO
IN THE SCHOOL PLAYGROUND IS WHERE THAT SHIT STARTS TO SHOW
THE OTHER KIDS WOULD PLAY HE-MAN AND GI JOE
BUT WHY I'D ASPIRE TO BE GI JOE I JUST DIDN'T KNOW
IT WAS KINDA CLEAR BY THEN THERE WAS A STRANGENESS WITHIN US
WE WERE MORE LIKE "YOU BE CHARLES MINGUS, I'LL BE STICKY FINGAZ"
I WAS A SCHOOL BOY STANDING IN A SCHOOL BOY STANCE
HURRY UP AND GIVE ME SOME SPACE TO GROW
SO I CAN I TRY TO ADVANCE

NOW JUST BECAUSE I DID NOT BECOME AN ASTRONAUT THAT DOES NOT MEAN THAT I HAVE FAILED NO NO NO NO NOT AT ALL IT SIMPLY MEANS THAT THE AMBITIONS OF A KID AT SCHOOL CAN BE RESTRICTED AND A LITTLE ONE DIMENSIONAL WE ARE ENCOURAGED TO PICK A JOB IN WHICH WE SEEK SUCCESS INSTEAD OF THINKING ABOUT WHAT WE REALLY NEED FOR HAPPINESS SO OUR GOAL BECOMES THAT JOB TITLE AND ANYTHING LESS IS DEEMED A FAILURE AND TO ME THAT IS QUITE HARD TO DIGEST

WHEN I GROW UP I WANT TO BE AN ASTRONAUT
MARRIED TO THE GIRL THROUGHOUT MY TEENS I HAD SOUGHT

Reading my dreams

THANKFULLY, not being a Beckham, I like to choose names for my poems that are somewhat relevant to the piece rather than their place of conception, otherwise the index of this book would just be a modified tube map.

I wrote this one night on the way home from a poetry gig in London. The buses and tube trains of London have been the birthplaces of many a verse.

I'd done a couple of poems that evening, along with many other open mic poets, and after watching a variety of poets I realised something: I generally write very dark poems! It occurred to me that it's good to push yourself out of your comfort zone so I decided to take on the daunting task of writing something that could be considered the polar opposite of "dark"!

The buses and tube trains of London have been the birthplaces of many a verse.

I had recently been introduced to the music of Vincent Oliver. If you haven't heard Vincent then you should really look into him. He has a very odd mixture of childlike innocence and caddish charm. He has a song called "If Yellow Were Sad", (from the album *EP 1*) and one line in it really stuck in my mind.

"I adjust to rest upon her sweet breast, and on her torso more so…"

This line was the foundation I used to write *Reading my Dreams*. I wanted to try and write what is essentially a love poem but without it seeming bland. I also didn't want to have any kind of twist or make it dark. I really wanted to stay out of my (dis) comfort zone.

In the end this became the hidden track on the first album I made with dan le sac, *Angles*. It worked nicely hidden away. A change from the norm but one that worked, I hope.

I received several submissions for this poem but the style and simplicity of this one won through. I loved how it all just allowed the poem to flow. And how each page linked together, thus connecting each piece of the journey travelled.

Damian Claughton

DAMIAN CLAUGHTON was born and brought up in Lincoln, England and showed a keen interest in art from an early age. He went on to study Graphic Design at Lincoln University before travelling around Asia for two years. On his return to the UK Damian moved to London where he works as a freelance Graphic Designer. He has recently started his own T-shirt range as a side project and his work can be viewed at www.myspace.com/mudahooka. His preferred weapons of choice are his camera and Mac.
mudahooka@yahoo.co.uk

Reading my Dreams

She's had such a long day and work has been stressful
As she arrives home to me weary and restful

To relax her I lead her to lay on the bed
And remove all the clothes from her waist to her head

I pray the emotion is taking effect

As I lay a kiss upon the nape of her neck

She rolls onto her back her eyes squinted and dreamy
As I gaze at her smile and the beauty beneath me

I adjust to rest upon her sweet breast
And on her torso more so

mudahooka

In each others arms and with interlocked hands
Lay two smiling faces and one set of plans

JUST A
BAND

JUST A BAND

Just
A
Band

Just
A BAND

JUST A BAND

JUST A
BAND

Just a band

JUST A BAND

just a band

JUST
A BAND

JUST / A B_AND

JUST A BAND.

The Just A Band design was created by Oliver Smith.

Magician's Assistant

WHEN I'm writing I like to use experiences from my life, whether it's something I've experienced directly or something I've observed close at hand. Sometimes, if it's a subject I don't have direct experience of, I will research and even interview people about it until I feel I understand the subject completely.

Then I go away and make something up!

This might sound strange but I have never felt it right to just take someone else's story and turn it into a piece. I like to create a new story instead, but one that is routed emotionally in reality.

In my life I have witnessed self-harm and suicide several times and it's always had a profound effect on me.

When I decided to write *Magician's Assistant* I was very conscious of making sure I gave the subject the respect it deserved while, at the same time, keeping true to my own feelings and beliefs (at the time of writing, at least).

I wanted to say in a poem what I hadn't had the chance to say, or maybe the bottle to say in real life. I needed to get across, not only, a level of understanding and empathy, but also a sense of the anger that I'd felt at the time.

I wanted to say in a poem what i hadn't had the chance, or maybe the bottle, to say in real life.

I remember the first time I performed the piece, aware that it was very dark, even for me. It was at a strange little festival (in Wimbledon I think) in an old historical ruin that had been sectioned off with an area for performing and another for the crowd. At the time I went on the crowd was probably out numbered by the other waiting poets (Musa Okwonga, Poeticat, Joshua Idehen and Inua Ellams to name but a few).

I decided to slip *Magician's Assistant* in as my second of three poems, figuring "if it doesn't go down well I could still end strong!"

And while it didn't exactly get a rousing applause (such subject matter seldom does and can often prove to be a real challenge for a crowd unsure how to react) the response I received from some of my fellow poets afterwards was enough to let me know I had done the subject at least some justice..

Inna Aizenshtein

INNA AIZENSHTEIN was born in Chisinau, Moldova. As a child, when she wasn't climbing trees or beating up boys, she was always with a pencil in her hand. Being interested in all kinds of art—including illustration, ceramics, even toy-making—it was clear she would always find a creative way to express herself.

In 2005, Inna graduated from Parsons School of Design in New York City with a BFA in Fine Art.

Inna now works in NYC as a fashion designer and illustrator.

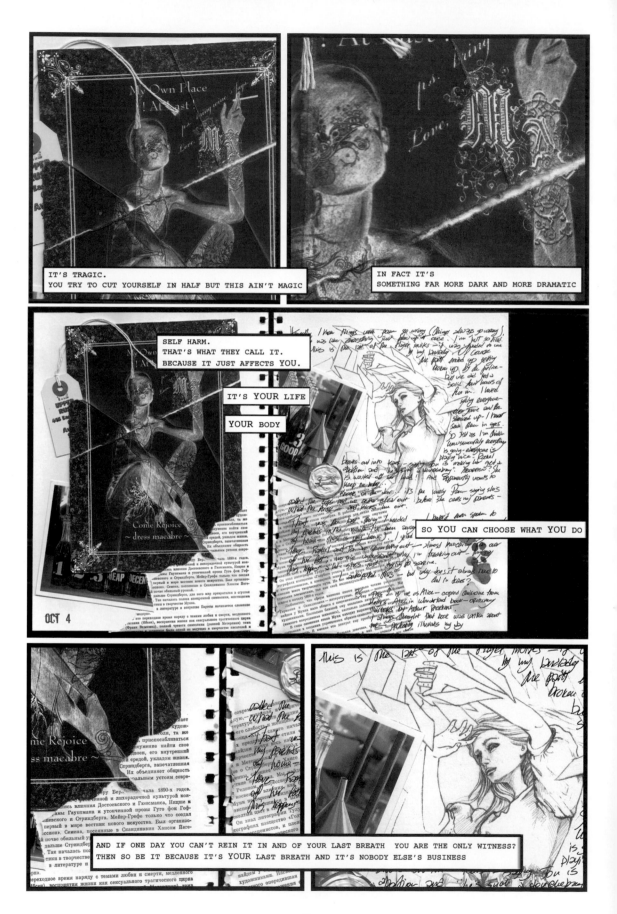

IT'S TRAGIC.
YOU TRY TO CUT YOURSELF IN HALF BUT THIS AIN'T MAGIC

IN FACT IT'S
SOMETHING FAR MORE DARK AND MORE DRAMATIC

SELF HARM.
THAT'S WHAT THEY CALL IT.
BECAUSE IT JUST AFFECTS YOU.

IT'S YOUR LIFE

YOUR BODY

SO YOU CAN CHOOSE WHAT YOU DO

AND IF ONE DAY YOU CAN'T REIN IT IN AND OF YOUR LAST BREATH YOU ARE THE ONLY WITNESS?
THEN SO BE IT BECAUSE IT'S YOUR LAST BREATH AND IT'S NOBODY ELSE'S BUSINESS

BUT... HOW ABOUT YOUR LITTLE SISTER?
I MEAN YOU THINK YOUR LIFE'S BEEN BAD
AND BY NO MEANS AM I BELITTLING THAT BECAUSE I KNOW THE TROUBLES YOU'VE HAD

BUT A TEEN FINDING OUT HER BIG SISTER CHOSE DEATH OVER LIFE
FINDING OUT THAT INSTEAD OF TURNING TO HER WITH YOUR PROBELMS, YOU TURNED TO A KNIFE

THAT'S A WHOLE LOT OF PAIN TO DEAL WITH, AND A WHOLE LOT OF DAMAGE
AND THE ONLY ROLE MODEL SHE HAS NOW IS LITTLE MORE THAN WORDS ENGRAVED IN GRANITE.

BUT AS YOU SAID BEFORE, THIS JUST AFFECTS YOU
IT'S YOUR LIFE
YOUR BODY
SO YOU CAN CHOOSE WHAT YOU DO
AND IF ONE DAY YOU CAN'T REIN IT IN AND OF YOUR LAST BREATH YOU ARE THE ONLY WITNESS?
THEN SO BE IT BECAUSE IT'S YOUR LAST BREATH AND IT'S NOBODY ELSE'S BUSINESS

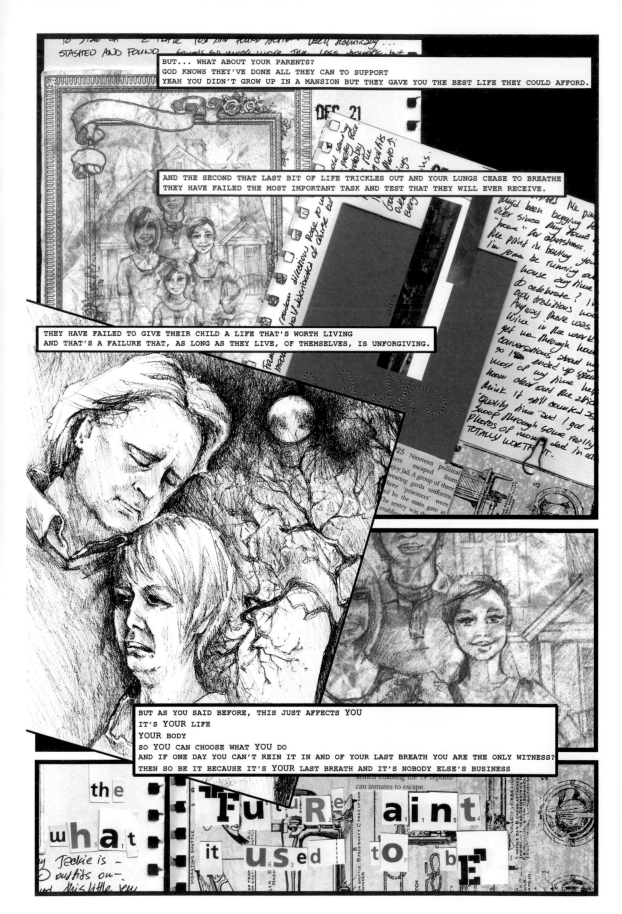

BUT... WHAT ABOUT YOUR PARENTS?
GOD KNOWS THEY'VE DONE ALL THEY CAN TO SUPPORT
YEAH YOU DIDN'T GROW UP IN A MANSION BUT THEY GAVE YOU THE BEST LIFE THEY COULD AFFORD.

AND THE SECOND THAT LAST BIT OF LIFE TRICKLES OUT AND YOUR LUNGS CEASE TO BREATHE
THEY HAVE FAILED THE MOST IMPORTANT TASK AND TEST THAT THEY WILL EVER RECEIVE.

THEY HAVE FAILED TO GIVE THEIR CHILD A LIFE THAT'S WORTH LIVING
AND THAT'S A FAILURE THAT, AS LONG AS THEY LIVE, OF THEMSELVES, IS UNFORGIVING.

BUT AS YOU SAID BEFORE, THIS JUST AFFECTS YOU
IT'S YOUR LIFE
YOUR BODY
SO YOU CAN CHOOSE WHAT YOU DO
AND IF ONE DAY YOU CAN'T REIN IT IN AND OF YOUR LAST BREATH YOU ARE THE ONLY WITNESS?
THEN SO BE IT BECAUSE IT'S YOUR LAST BREATH AND IT'S NOBODY ELSE'S BUSINESS

the what FuTuRe aint it uSed to be

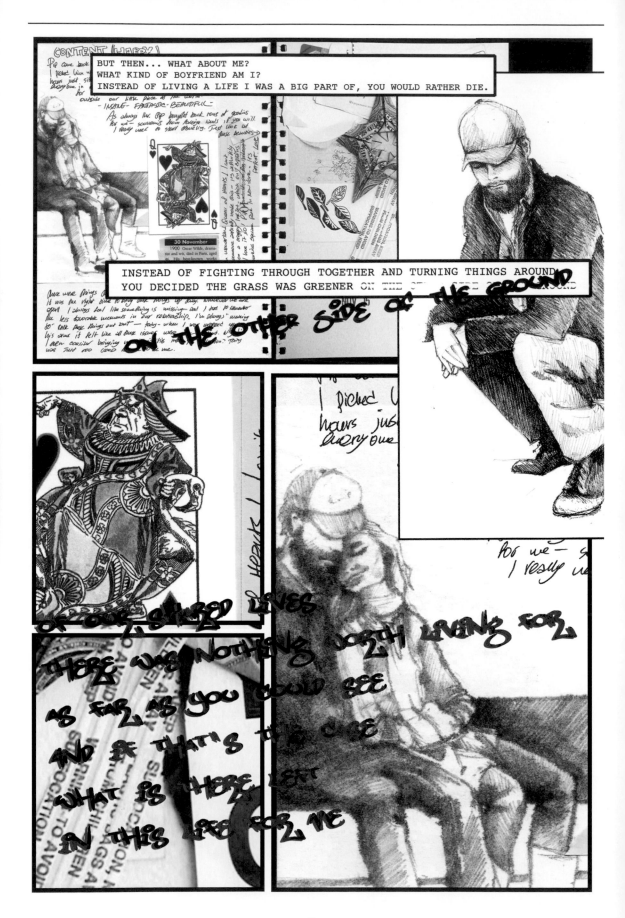

BUT THEN... WHAT ABOUT ME?
WHAT KIND OF BOYFRIEND AM I?
INSTEAD OF LIVING A LIFE I WAS A BIG PART OF, YOU WOULD RATHER DIE.

INSTEAD OF FIGHTING THROUGH TOGETHER AND TURNING THINGS AROUND
YOU DECIDED THE GRASS WAS GREENER ON THE OTHER SIDE OF THE GROUND

ON THE OTHER SIDE OF THE GROUND

OF OUR SHARED LIVES
THERE WAS NOTHING WORTH LIVING FOR
AS FAR AS YOU COULD SEE
AND IF THAT'S THE CASE
WHAT IS THERE LEFT
IN THIS LIFE FOR ME

BUT AS YOU SAID BEFORE

THIS JUST AFFECTS YOU

ITS YOUR LIFE

YOUR BODY

YOUR SISTER

YOUR PARENTS

YOUR FRIENDS

AND YOUR PARTNER

SO YOU CAN CHOOSE WHAT YOU DO

AND IF ONE DAY YOU CANT REIN IT

IN AND OF YOUR LAST BREATH

YOU ARE THE ONLY WITNESS

THEN FUCK EVERYBODY ELSE

BECAUSE THAT AINT SOMETHING

YOUVE GOT TO LIVE WITH

EMMA'S JOURNAL
12

IF FOUND PLEASE CALL
76 76 834

PiP

Ode to a b-boy

IN 2002 I lost a really good friend of mine. I had met Jaimie at college and we just seemed to get on. Musical tastes, we clicked. Sense of humour, we clicked.

When he passed away, it really seemed to come out of nowhere.

At times like that, everyone questions if there was anything they could have done differently, or if their time together could have been better spent, but those sorts of questions can never be answered and are, of course, completely futile.

A lot of what I did after 2002 was, in my mind, done in some way to honour Jaimie. It's hard not to become completely driven and self-motivated when you have seen someone with so much creativity and potential bow out in their prime. So when I started creeping around the streets at night spraying stencils on walls, it's not surprising the first stencil I made was of Jaimie.

But it wasn't a subject I felt I could write about straight away. And even though I do tend to write about death and dark subject matters quite a bit, this one just didn't feel right.

when you lose someone they become frozen in time.

When I finally decided to write *Ode to a B-Boy* I chose to write not about Jaimie's passing itself, but about how things had changed in that time. When you lose someone they become frozen in time. A perfect image, never ageing, never falling from grace. While those left alive grow older, develop and change.

It left me wondering what Jaimie would make of the me now. I wasn't Scroobius Pip back then when I knew Jaimie, I was Dave and I wasn't writing or being that creative back then either, I was out getting drunk and listening to anything that was loud. And even though I know this is another of those unanswerable, futile questions it is one that made me realise that it's ok to grow and change and move on with your life.

I've been lucky to share my time, so far, on this planet with some great people. Some of them have left too soon but all of them have had some kind of impact on me, whether great or small, personal or peripheral.

So along with Jaimie, this is dedicated to Natalie/Frank and Sam/Goo.

CJ McCracken

CJ MCCRACKEN (aka Zombiehamster) is a comic book artist and writer, currently residing on the outskirts of Bedlam and Squalor. When not hiding in his studio, hunched over a drawing table, he can be tracked down on his website; zombiehamster.com.

He has been known to appear occasionally in public brandishing bags of obscure vinyl recordings and releases odd little mixtapes on a somewhat regular basis. He is the creator of *Godzilla Boy* and *Mugwump*, but please don't hold that against him. To contact, email: cjmccracken@gmail.com

We used to try and freak each other out and, that night, I decided to just stare at you for as long as I could. Every time you looked round I'd appear from somewhere staring. Some people would only have the patience to keep that kind of rubbish up for half an hour or so. Not you and me though. We could make stuff like that last a whole night out.

I know you found it amusing at the time.

We both did.

I remember. With hindsight though, I wouldn't have bothered.

I would have just grabbed a drink and proceeded to the dance floor

Let you win this one. But that's hindsight for you.

And I'm not one to dwell on things these days. I don't feel bad that I've got used to you not being here.

...Time does that I guess.

waiting for the beat to kick in

OF all the pieces I've written over the years, this is one that I've always been particularly proud of. It appeared as the last track on the le sac vs pip album *Angles* and both dan and I have always picked it as one of our favourites. I think this is partly because it's not one we play live and so hasn't been tarnished by being performed night after night!

I really enjoyed the freedom of writing such a long, winding piece. It drifts between rhyming couplets and straight narrative and really seems to get across the vibe of a journey. It also allowed the movie geek in me to get out. All the characters in this piece are based on and named after characters from some of my favourite films (Elwood P Dowd – *Harvey*, Lloyd Dobler – *Say Anything*, Billy Brown – *Buffalo '66*, Walter Neff – *Double Indemnity*). With this poem I wanted to get across the ways in which different films have genuinely influenced my outlook on life.

i really enjoyed the freedom of writing such a long, winding piece.

I really think that the art of cinema, mainstream included, is a truly underrated art form; it seems to be seen primarily as a form of temporary entertainment but I firmly believe that films can be just as moving and educational as any other form of art.

From the day I started this project I had hoped someone would take this piece on, but week after week, month after month, I received nothing. Largely, I imagine, due to it being so long and with no guarantee of making it into the final collection, I could understand why no one seemed to be willing.

I had almost resigned myself to the fact that it wasn't to be when I received an email titled *Waiting for the Beat to Kick In.* I was obviously delighted. All the same though, I prepared myself to be disappointed. Would it be good enough to be dragged into the folder marked "finalists", I pondered. Most of the poems had received several submissions, of varying standards. So I took a deep breath and opened the email and was thrilled. This was a STRONG submission. The noir approach perfectly fitted the world I had imagined.

Quickly I acted.

Click. Drag. Accidentally drop in the deleted folder. Click again. Drag again. Drop in the "finalists" folder.

Matt Frodsham

MATT FRODSHAM is a designer, illustrator and animator from Warrington, currently working internationally from Manchester and Liverpool creating graphic and motion design. He studied Graphic Design at Salford University, but now much prefers to make things move and tell stories (this book is a happy medium!).

His motion work can be seen at www.vimeo.com/mattfrodsham and he can be contacted at mattfrodsham@gmail.com

I WAS WALKING ALONG THROUGH UNFAMILIAR STREETS AND IT FELT STRANGE BECAUSE THERE DIDN'T SEEM TO BE ANYONE ELSE AROUND

I DIDN'T KNOW WHERE I WAS BUT IT HAD THE FEEL OF NEW YORK. BUT NOT NEW YORK IN REAL LIFE, THE NEW YORK YOU SEE IN OLD FILMS

I CAN'T REALLY EXPLAIN WHY BUT IT JUST HAD THAT VIBE, EVERY STEP I TOOK FELT SOMEHOW MORE DRAMATIC

SO I KEPT ON WALKING AND THEN, DOWN AN ALLEY, BEHIND A BAR, SITTING ON SOME METAL STEPS I SAW A MAN.

FROM THE LOOK AND SMELL OF HIM IT WAS CLEAR HE ENJOYED A DRINK BUT HE WASN'T IN SUCH A STATE THAT I FELT HIM TO BE ANY KIND OF IRRATIONAL THREAT SO I APPROACHED HIM....

AH, MR PIP....

HE SAID OUT LOUD

WE'VE BEEN AWAITING YOU, MY NAME IS *ELWOOD P DOWD*

NOW JUST WHAT HE MEANT BY "WE" I DIDN'T REALLY GET, BUT ALL THE SAME I TOOK A SEAT NEXT TO HIM ON THE STEP

HE SAID...

YOU'LL MEET A FEW PEOPLE BEFORE THIS DAY IS THROUGH WHO WILL ADMINISTER ADVICE AND GUIDELINES FOR YOU

NOW WHAT EACH OF US WILL SAY I'LL TELL YOU NOW IS TRUE, BUT WHETHER OR NOT YOU TAKE THIS ADVICE IS FOR YOU TO CHOOSE

AT THAT POINT HE ACTED LIKE SOMEONE HAD WHISPERED IN HIS EAR, WHICH, SINCE NO—ONE ELSE WAS THERE, WAS PRETTY DAMN WEIRD

AWKWARDLY I LOOKED AWAY AND KINDA PLAYED WITH MY BEARD, HE CLEARED HIS THROAT FOR A SECOND THEN SAID...

LISTEN HERE

WITH THIS INFORMATION I WAS ENCOURAGED TO WALK ON.

I CONTINUED ALONE THROUGH THESE EMPTY STREETS THINKING OVER WHAT ELWOOD HAD SAID BUT AT THE SAME TIME THINKING ABOUT HOW FUCKING WEIRD THIS DAY HAD BEEN SO FAR.

I WAS IN MY OWN LITTLE WORLD WHEN A HAND WAS PLACED ON MY CHEST AND A GUY SAID....

LOOK OUT, THERE'S SOME BROKEN GLASS ON THE FLOOR THERE

I LOOKED UP AND HE SAID....

HI, PLEASED TO MEET YOU MY NAME IS LLOYD DOBLER, I'LL GET STRAIGHT TO THE POINT, WON'T TAKE TO MUCH TIME FROM YA

I'M PROBABLY THE YOUNGEST PERSON YOU'LL GET ADVICE FROM TODAY AND YOU MAY THINK A GUY OF MY AGE WOULDN'T HAVE ANYTHING TO SAY

BUT IT'S SAID THAT OBSERVATION, NOT OLD AGE, BRINGS WISDOM. AND I OBSERVE EVERY LIFE LESSON I'M GIVEN

BUT I WON'T ATTEMPT TO TELL YOU HOW TO LOVE OR HOW TO BE LOVED, CO'Z YOU GET A DIFFERENT GENIE EACH TIME THAT PARTICULAR LANTERN IS RUBBED

...BUT I WILL OFFER ADVICE ON DEALING WITH LIFE ITS UPS AND ITS DOWNS, ITS TROUBLES AND ITS STRIFE

...AND THEN JUST BE IN A GOOD MOOD?

THAT'S ALL I HAVE TO SAY BECAUSE IT'S A STRAIGHT UP FACT. YOU CONTROL YOUR EMOTIONS AND IT'S AS SIMPLE AS THAT

HE WALKED OFF THEN, LEAVING ME TO CONTEMPLATE THIS BRIEF ENCOUNTER I HAD BARELY HAD TIME TO REALISE I WAS BEING TAUGHT SOMETHING BEFORE HE WAS GONE.

ON I WALKED AND, ALMOST IMMEDIATELY I SPOTTED MY NEXT GUIDE IT COULDN'T BE CLEARER.

THIS GUY WAS STANDING ON THE STREET CORNER PACING BACK AND FORTH...

SKINNY LOOKING
GUY, LEATHER
JACKET,
TIGHT JEANS,
RETRO LOOK.

I'VE RARELY SEEN
SOMEONE LOOK
QUITE SO
UNCOMFORTABLE
IN THEIR OWN SKIN
TWITCHING,
SMOOTHING HIS
HAIR BACK,
KICKING AT THE
FLOOR, LOOKING
UP AND DOWN THE
STREET.

HE CLEARLY DIDN'T
ENJOY WAITING
AROUND SO I
APPROACHED HIM
QUICKLY TO PUT
HIM OUT OF HIS
MISERY AND LET
HIM START HIS
SCHPEEL

HI MY NAME IS
BILLY BROWN AND I
AIN'T GONNA GIVE YOU SOME
QUOTE INSTEAD I'M GONNA
USE SOME STUFF THAT
YOU WROTE

ALWAYS HAD THE FEELING
I COULD NEVER BE THE
VILLAIN COZ THE VILLAIN
IN THE FILMS
IS ALWAYS
BACKLIT

NOW I FIND IT PLEASING TO DEFEND MYSELF WITH REASON BUT THE CLOCK IS ALWAYS SITTING ON MY BACK

TICK TICK TICK TICK

THEN?

NO EXPLOSION BUT PERSISTENCE BRINGS EROSION

LIKE A PICTURE THAT'S BEEN OVER OVERLY EXPOSED

AND LIKE A FOX THAT'S BEEN RAN OVER IN THE ROAD AND... ROAD AND... ROAD AND

BASICALLY WHAT I'M TRYING TO SAY TO YOU IS YOU DON'T ACHIEVE ANYTHING BY LETTING THE PAST DWELL WITHIN YOU

GETTING ALL PENT UP AND ANGRY ABOUT THIS STUFF JUST EATS AWAY INSIDE YOU

WHAT'S THAT OTHER LINE OF YOURS?

"IF YOU CAN'T FORGIVE AND FORGET, HOW'S THIS? FORGET FORGIVING AND JUST ACCEPT, THEN THAT'S IT."

SEE THAT'S HOW ITS GOTTA BE THEN YOU CAN FALL IN LOVE, GET ON WITH YOUR LIFE AND BE FREE

ALMOST BEFORE HE HAD EVEN FINISHED THAT SENTENCE HE WAS OFF DOWN THE ROAD HIS HANDS IN HIS POCKETS AS HE HURRIED AWAY

NOW, QUITE ACCEPTING OF THE TOTALLY SURREAL TIME I WAS HAVING, I ROUNDED THE CORNER AND CONTINUED ON TO MY NEXT ENCOUNTER.

RESIGNED TO THE FACT THIS WAS SOME KIND OF DREAM OR HALLUCINATION I MADE MY WAY THROUGH THIS NOW DARK STREET TO THE ONE WINDOW THAT HAD A LIGHT ON.

I WALKED THROUGH THE UNLOCKED DOOR WHICH, INCIDENTALLY, HAD BLINDS DOWN AND A SILHOUETTED FIGURE LIKE A FILM NOIR SCENE BUT SADLY NO SIGN SAYING "PRIVATE EYE"

AS I ENTERED A TIRED VOICE PROMPTLY SAID

THIS JOURNEYS ALMOST OVER; I'M THE ONLY ONE LEFT ALLOW ME TO INTRODUCE MYSELF, THE NAMES WALTER NEFF

THE OTHER GUYS HAVE TAUGHT YOU THINGS OF GREAT POSITIVE WORTH BUT I'M AFRAID I AM HERE TO BRING YOU DOWN TO EARTH

SEE YOU CAN LIVE YOUR LIFE IN CONTROL AND BE NICE BUT EVEN THAT WILL NOT PROMISE YOU A HAPPY LIFE

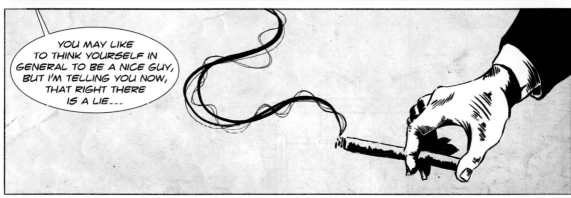

YOU MAY LIKE TO THINK YOURSELF IN GENERAL TO BE A NICE GUY, BUT I'M TELLING YOU NOW, THAT RIGHT THERE IS A LIE...

EVEN THE NICEST OF GUYS HAVE GOT SOME *NASTY* WITHIN THEM...

YOU DON'T HAVE TO BE BACKLIT TO BE THE VILLAIN

WHETHER IT BE GREED, LUST OR JUST PLAIN VINDICTIVENESS, THERE'S A LEVEL OF MALEVOLENCE INSIDE ALL OF US

SO YOU CAN PAINT YOURSELF AN IMAGE AND LIVE IN YOUR OWN LITTLE DREAM. BUT THIS AIN'T A DREAM, THIS IS ONE BIG SILVER SCREEN

SO YOU'LL BE WAITING FOR
THE BEAT TO KICK IN
BUT IT NEVER DOES

WAITING FOR MY FEET
TO GROW WINGS
THAT LIFT ME ABOVE

ALL OF THESE
TIRESOME THINGS
THAT WE KNOW AND LOVE

WAITING FOR THE BEAT
TO KICK IN
BUT IT NEVER DOES...

Thou shalt Always kill

WELL this is the big one really, isn't it!

I wrote this piece a while back and always used to end my spoken word sets with it.

I performed it for the first time at an open mic night, run by Niall O'Sullivan, called *Poetry Unplugged* at the poetry café in Covent Garden. A posh couple sat in the crowd talking loudly over everyone else's poems. I was scheduled to go on late, right after the male half of this couple. He got up and recited an ancient Latin poem he had recently translated. I personally found it very underwhelming but he seemed very pleased with himself.

I followed him with two short poems and ended on *Thou Shalt Always Kill* with the key addition of: "Thou shalt not spend the whole night talking through everyone else's performance then get up and recite a poem you didn't even write yourself!"

And that is the beauty of list poems!
You can normally update them with ease.

there was a lot of sweating going on in those early recordings!

When dan le sac and I started working together he sent me a beat that seemed perfect for this poem. I was living with my mum at the time and my "recording studio" was a pretty basic 16-track desk that I kept under clothes in my bedroom. When recording I would wear four big wool hats to try and stop the sound leaking from my cheap headphones onto the recording. It wasn't exactly a "professional" set up and there was a lot of sweating going on in those early recordings! Within an hour or two of receiving the beat I had shuffled the lines about, added the "Just a Band" section, recorded the vocal in my bedroom and emailed it back to dan. He tweaked it a bit and emailed it back. In the next few weeks we posted it on MySpace and talked to a friend of dan's (Nick Frew) about a video, and I sent a CDR of the track to John Kennedy at *XFM*. Within hours of receiving it he played it on his show and launched us from our bedrooms into the bedrooms of people all over the country.

Nick Frew then masterfully made a video for the princely sum of £200 that we posted up on YouTube and it went on to have around three million views.

That over-excited, under-practiced bedroom recording ended up being used on the original release, the video and being the catalyst for everything that came after.

Ben Williams

BEN WILLIAMS aka Beachbum decided to let his friends choose what he should say about himself and this is what they came up with. He's not sure what it says about him but he supposes it's his own fault really.
"Ben has had a string of lovely girlfriends from other countries."

Thou shalt not steal if there is a direct victim;

Thou shalt not worship pop idols or follow lost prophets;

Thou shalt not take the names of Johnny Cash, Joe Strummer, Johnny Hartman, Desmond Dekker, Jim Morrison, Jimi Hendrix or Syd Barrat in vain;

Thou shalt not think that any male over 30 that plays with a child that is not their own is a paedophile, some people are just nice;

Thou shalt not read NME;

Thou shalt not stop liking a band just because they have become popular;

Thou shalt not question Stephen Fry;

Thou shalt not judge a book by its cover;

Thou shalt not judge Lethal Weapon by Danny Glover;

Thou shalt not buy Coca Cola products;

Thou shalt not buy nestle products;

Thou shalt not go into the woods with your boyfriend bestfriend, take drugs and cheat on him;

Thou shalt not fall in love so easily;

Thou shalt not use poetry, art or music to get into girl's pants ......use it to get into their heads;

Thou shalt not watch HOLLYOAKS;

Thou shalt not attend an open mic and then leave as soon as you have done your shitty little poem or song you self righteous prick;

Thou shalt not return to the same club or bar week in & week out just because you once saw a girl there that you fancied that you're never going to talk to anyway;

Thou shalt not put musicians and recording artists on ridiculous pedestals no matter how great they are or were;

Thou shalt give equal worth to tragedies that occur in non english speaking countries as to those that occur in english speaking countries;

Thou shalt remember that guns, bitches and bling 1 2 3 4 $ were never part of the four elements and never will be;

Thou shalt not make repetitive generic music,
Thou shalt not make repetitive generic music,
Thou shalt not make repetitive generic music,
Thou shalt not make repetitive generic music,

Thou shalt not pimp my ride;

Thou shalt not scream if you wanna go faster;

Thou shalt not move to the sound of the wickedness;

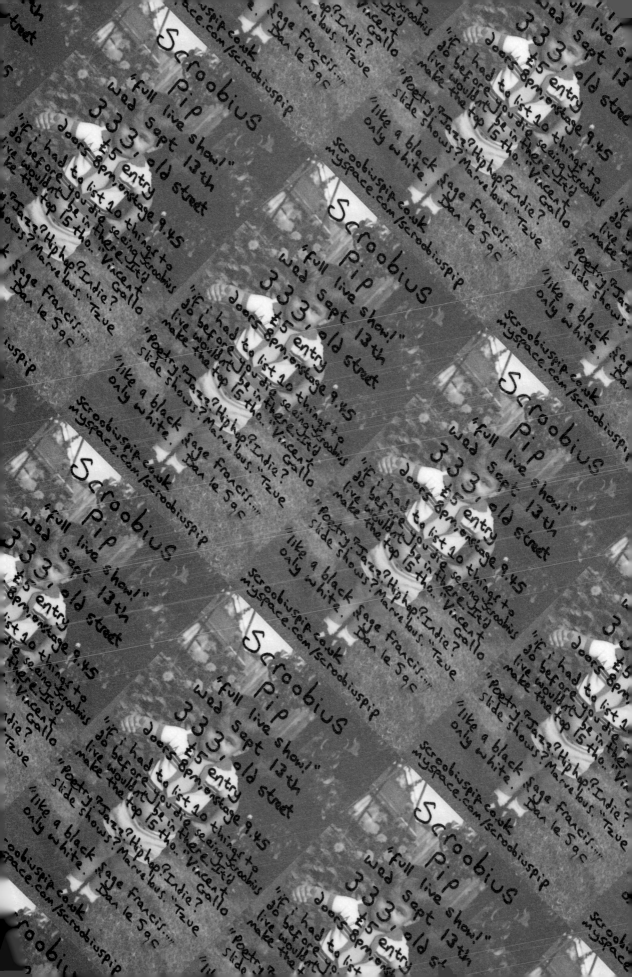

Shamed

WHEN I was about sixteen I ran away from home in a very misjudged teenage angst act of rebellion. I think I may have stayed out two nights at best/worst. To really perpetuate the teenage angst vibe I took my acoustic guitar.

I stayed in hostels in London and generally wandered the streets. At one point, I was sat in Covent Garden and someone threw me some money, assuming I was busking. That simple kind act made me feel really guilty; I obviously didn't NEED to be there and I had places I could go. But there were people living on the streets that really needed that money and had nowhere else to go.

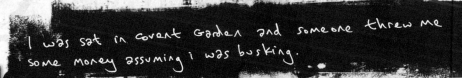

I was sat in covent garden and someone threw me some money assuming i was busking.

Years later this all sprung back to mind when I decided, as an exercise, to write some short poems about different emotions. One of the emotions I chose was shame. I started to think about all the homeless people who live on our streets. About how some of them MUST have families and loved ones out there somewhere. I tried to imagine what might force me into a similar situation and I decided that the only thing that might stop me from being able to go home or look my loved ones in the eye would be an overwhelming sense of shame.

Shame is a hugely powerful emotion and tied to pride; it can be one of the hardest things to overcome. It's an emotion that becomes more difficult, not easier, to deal with, the more we respect or love those closest to us.

When this artist, Mister Paterson, first got in touch from his MySpace page, I decided to check out some of his artwork. One of the things I noticed was that the characters he drew tended to have tattoos and I wondered what kind of characters he would include in his submission.

When I received his entry I was both pleased and surprised. Not only did tattoos play a major part in his artwork, but I also really liked the way Mister Paterson used the initial image of the tattooed man as a panel to tell the rest of the story in.

Mister Paterson

Born in a rainy town in 1978 MISTER PATERSON began painting at the age of two, when he created his first masterpiece, entitled "Parent's fireplace...in green". Apparently he took it upon himself to liberally coat the fireplace in a vibrant lime green paint the day his parents were due to move out. In his 31 years he has continued to work with the same spontaneity, moving from project to project.

"I've never settled on one thing, I paint, draw, sculpt, make music and just recently started learning how to tattoo, which fits in nicely with my work."

Having failed most subjects at school except art he took time to pursue "loafing" before finally getting his act together and going on to obtain an art degree at Manchester Metropolitan University. He has been working freelance ever since.

www.dontstopcreating.com (Official site)
www.misterpatersonartist@myspace.com

I'm shamed

and at 36 ive got a bed full of cans.

I'm shamed by the fact that, sometimes, I find humour in this Instead of the perpetual shame that should exsist

I'm shamed by the people that look at me
and it ruins their day
I'm shamed by the people that notice me
and just choose to look away

I'm shamed by the kids last night that thought it
was fun to hit me with a football

And I'm shamed by the millions of people that
don't notice me at all.

I'm shamed because I haven't seen my
son in years
I'm shamed because, if he walked past me,
I'd just hide away in tears

I'm shamed by the lack of shame I have
when pushed to my limits
I'm shamed by the sleeping bag I call my
home and the possessions within it

Rat Race

FROM around 2002 to 2006 I worked in a record shop.

When I first applied for the job I imagined it would be like working in the record shops of High Fidelity or Empire Records. After a month or two of rabid Christmas shoppers, I realised this wasn't going to be the case.

The free-spirited, music-loving vibe was replaced by the drone of pop charts, new release playlists, stock counts, stock checks, stock rooms and stock greetings. So it may be surprising to hear that I look back on those four years with nothing but fond memories.

Whilst the hours were long, at times painful, and the tasks often mundane, the people I happened to be coupled with were, on the whole, pretty good! I went on to develop some amazing friendships (and of course, one or two bitter rivalries).

what in the world is more 'real' than writing about your boring job?

At the first branch I worked in one member of the management team (known now only as loyal husband, father of two and producer extraordinaire... FlamesYall) was a huge hip-hop fan. We would exchange favourite lines and recommends daily. Within a few months we had learned that the best way to pass our time was to pen raps on the backs of till receipts while we went about our tasks. These of course started out as petty, childish attacks on anyone and everyone (purely for comedy effect, you understand), although over time the comedy diss raps started to run thin and we wound up writing longer and more developed pieces.

We had discovered that, for all the pitfalls of a mundane, unchallenging job, there was also a glaring advantage we had overlooked. Doing a job that consists largely of waiting to serve people or stocking shelves provides you with hour upon hour of spare "head time" and we both started to write and develop full verses during our shifts.

Rat Race was one of the first such pieces. Hip hop as a genre has often banged on about "keeping it real", so I figured, "What in the world is more 'real' than writing about your boring job whilst actually doing your boring job..."

CowFree
Illustrator/Animator/Angry Person.
Stop shopping.
Thanks.
Myspace.com/cowpatlicker
Cow_free@hotmail.co.uk

AND WHAT'S WORSE STILL I'VE LOST MY MAP SO I DON'T KNOW WHERE THIS SHIT ENDS AH SHIT. I'M BACK IN THE RAT RACE AGAIN.

STAFF ONLY

AS I WAKE UP WITH THE PREVIOUS NIGHT STILL RINGING IN MY FRAGILE HEAD TRYING TO PIECE TOGETHER ANY SHITTY THINGS I MIGHT OF DONE OR MIGHT OF SAID I DRAG MY LIFELESS CARCASS TO ITS FEET AND OUT OF BED AND CLOCK IN TO ANOTHER DAY.

FRESH INT

ANOTHER DAY WHERE I CAN LOOK FORWARD TO THE POSSIBILITY THAT MAYBE TODAY WILL BE THE DAY THAT SOMETHING INTERRUPTS THE NEVER-ENDING LIST OF MUNDANE TASKS THAT SIT BETWEEN ME AND THE CLOSING BRACKETS OF MY DRIVE HOME.

MAYBE TODAY WILL BE THE DAY THAT SOMETHING SNAPS AS I THINK BACK AND REACT TO THE DISTINCT LACK OF IMPACT IN MY SHRINK-WRAPPED LIFE.

MAY BE TODAY WILL BE THE DAY I TEAR DOWN THE FOUNDATIONS OF MY WHOLE EXSISTENCE AND START AGAIN. KNEE DEEP IN RUBBLE. RUMMAGING FOR SOMETHING I CAN USE AS A STARTING POINT TO REBUILD. SOMETHING TO JUMP OFF OF.

BUT THEN..... THE FUTURE AIN'T WHAT IT USED TO BE AND AS THE DAY'S TASKS REVERBERATE AROUND MY DORMANT BRAIN I CONTINUE TO WELCOME ANOTHER MEMBER OF PUBLIC WITH A PERFECT REPLICA OF WHAT IS KNOWN AS A WELCOMING SMILE.

BUT BEFORE LONG MY CREATIVE NIGHTMARE IS INTERRUPTED BY THE EVER WATCHING EYES OF MY SUPERIORS.

BBTV

COZ LIKE A CHILD SPINNING IN CIRCLES JUST TO MAKE HIMSELF DIZZY MY ONLY REAL REQUIREMENT IN THIS PLACE IS TO MAKE SURE I **LOOK** BUSY.

WELCOME TO HUCKOS

BUT I'M USING THAT TO MY ADVANTAGE. YOU SEE JUST AS EVERY OPEN EYE IS NOT SEEING, NOT EVERY CLOSED EYE IS SLEEPING. SO ALTHOUGH THEY PAY ME FOR THIS PAINTED BY NUMBERS SHIT EVERY I'M LEEPING I HAVE AND REMEMBER THE SAME SHIT CAN TASTE PRETTY FUCKING DIFFERENT IF THEY SEASON IT RIGHT. SO IF YOUR GOING TO SELL OUT YOUR BELIEFS MAKE SURE YOUR REASONS ARE WATER TIGHT.

AND AS THE CHIEF WORKER BEE TRIES HIS BEST TO NURTURE ME AND SEARCHES DEEP TO HELP ME FIND THE KEY THAT MIGHT JUST UNLOCK AND HELP ME FREE THE INNER BOURGEOISIE THAT WITH TIME AND EFFORT I COULD SOMEDAY BE TAKING BULLET POINT STEPS FROM A-Z, LEAPING OVER THE BORING PARTS LIKE A CORPORATE FLEA I LOOK AT MY SUPPOSED LUMINARY AND I SIMPLY DON'T AGREE.

I AM THE EMPLOYEE OF THE MONTH

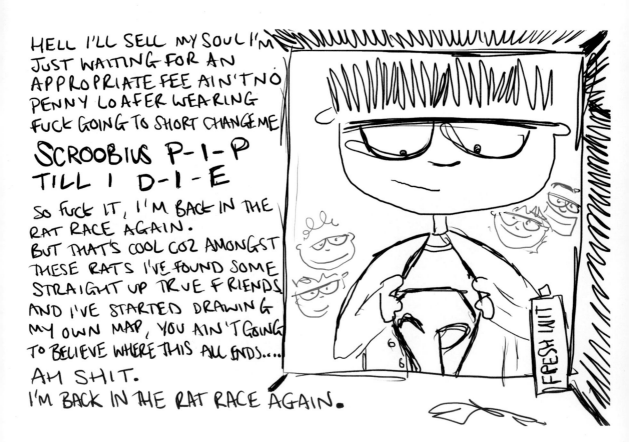

HELL I'LL SELL MY SOUL I'M JUST WAITING FOR AN APPROPRIATE FEE AIN'T NO PENNY LOAFER WEARING FUCK GOING TO SHORT CHANGE ME

SCROOBIUS P-I-P TILL I D-I-E

SO FUCK IT, I'M BACK IN THE RAT RACE AGAIN. BUT THAT'S COOL COZ AMONGST THESE RATS I'VE FOUND SOME STRAIGHT UP TRUE FRIENDS AND I'VE STARTED DRAWING MY OWN MAP, YOU AIN'T GOING TO BELIEVE WHERE THIS ALL ENDS.....

AH SHIT.

I'M BACK IN THE RAT RACE AGAIN.

FRESH WIT

Scroobius Pip, Rat Race 2009 by Tom Harris, Biro on paper, 210 x 297cm.